Gun Control

DEBATING
THE ISSUES

Gun Control

Cavendish
Square

New York

RUTH
BJORKLUND

Published in 2014 by Cavendish Square Publishing, LLC
303 Park Avenue South, Suite 1247, New York, NY 10010

Library of Congress Cataloging-in-Publication Data

Bjorklund, Ruth.
Gun control / Ruth Bjorklund.
  p. cm. — (Debating the issues)
Includes bibliographical references and index.
Summary: "Examines the two sides of the debate related to gun control including policies and practices
throughout American history, gun laws and legislation, gun safety, and crime and law enforcement"—
Provided by publisher.
ISBN 978-1-62712-416-4 (hardcover) ISBN 978-1-62712-417-1 (paperback) ISBN 978-1-62712-418-8
(ebook)
1. Gun control—United States—Juvenile literature. 2. Firearms—Law and legislation—United States—
Juvenile literature. 3. Violent crimes—United States—Juvenile literature. 4. Firearms ownership—
Government policy—United States—Juvenile literature. I. Title.
HV7436.B56 2013
363.330973—dc23
2011046113

Editor: Peter Mavrikis
Art Director: Anahid Hamparian
Series design by Sonia Chaghatzbanian
Production Manager: Jennifer Ryder-Talbot
Production Editor: Andrew Coddington

Photo research by Alison Morretta

Table of Contents

Chapter 1

The History of Gun Control in America

The Second Amendment to the United States Constitution reads as follows:

> A well regulated militia, being necessary to the security of a free State, the right of the people to keep and bear Arms, shall not be infringed.

The Framers of the Constitution never intended for any part of this document to be obscure, but the wording of the Second Amendment has long been considered ambiguous. As a result, Americans have been divided over how to interpret their Second Amendment right to possess firearms. Those who **advocate** gun control and limitations on the right to bear arms and those who are supporters of unrestricted gun-ownership rights generally disagree about the meaning of the language as it was written in the eighteenth century, and the discord between the two factions has grown in the twentieth and twenty-first centuries. Those who drafted the Bill of Rights were clearly establishing a right to keep and bear arms, but the extent of the right and to whom it applies are still in dispute.

Before considering the conflict of opinions between proponents of gun control and proponents of gun rights, it is important to review

A six-cylinder revolver rests on a copy of the U.S. Constitution.

the history of **firearms** in the United States and to be familiar with the historical context of the Second Amendment and its language.

History

After the American colonies successfully fought and won their independence from England, American statesmen set to the task of establishing the responsibilities and the functions of the new federal government. They drafted a constitution to be ratified by the thirteen original states. The document's many opponents, who were called anti-Federalists, believed that the proposed constitution would give too much power to the federal government and, further, that it did not provide adequate provisions for individual liberties. For agreeing to ratify the Constitution, the anti-Federalists were promised that amendments granting specific liberties and rights would follow. The first ten of these amendments are collectively called the Bill of Rights.

The authors of the Second Amendment were addressing two principles: that the state may call upon an armed citizen **militia** to safeguard it against sudden attack or abusive government, and that the people have the right to own firearms. Whether it is only members of regulated citizen militias, collectively referred to as "the people," who have the right to keep and bear arms or whether "the people" refers to all individual persons has been at the crux of many decades of debate. The thirteen original states each addressed the issue in their state constitutions. Some were more specific in their language. Pennsylvania and Vermont, for example, favored individual rights to gun ownership,

A statue in Lexington, Massachusetts, honors a citizen-militia captain who fought in the American Revolution.

extending to both individuals and the state: "the right of the citizens to bear arms in defense of themselves and the State shall not be questioned." Massachusetts and Virginia emphasized the people's right to possess firearms in order to participate in a state militia. (Members of militias were expected to supply their own weapons.) The Massachusetts constitution states, "The people have a right to keep and bear arms for the common defense," and the Virginia state constitution further states, "That a well trained militia, composed of the body of the people, trained to arms, is the proper, natural, and safe defense of a Free State; that standing armies, in times of peace, should be avoided, as dangerous to liberty…"

Since the Second Amendment was ratified on December 15, 1791, a number of laws and court rulings have sought to clarify its meaning or define its scope. One year after signing the amendment, lawmakers passed the first gun-control law, which made it illegal for African slaves to possess firearms. After the Civil War, many southern states, including Alabama, Tennessee, and Texas, passed gun-control laws restricting the sale of any gun except very expensive army and navy pistols. These laws effectively denied poor people the ability to purchase guns. By 1850, as America expanded, most of the new western states and territories did not allow concealed weapons. In many small towns, guns had to be left with a sheriff or checked in at the door of a public building. In the mid-nineteenth century, Samuel Colt was awarded a patent for a pistol he called the Colt **revolver**. Unlike the handguns of the day, this handgun did not require reloading after one or two bullets were shot. The Colt revolver could shoot five or six bullets in a row. Colt and other gun makers, such as Smith & Wesson, began manufacturing automatic rifles. The popularity of these automatic firearms grew, and gun manufacturers soon were able to sell their products more cheaply. Many people became concerned that there was too much firepower available to too many untrained gun owners.

After an assassination attempt in New York City in 1911 on Mayor William Gaynor, the state legislature passed a law, the Sullivan Act,

Gun laws enacted after the Civil War restricted handgun ownership to people who could afford expensive weapons such as this Colt army revolver.

which required persons to have a permit to own and carry a pistol. After World War I, Americans living in urban areas became more concerned about an increase in crime. By 1924, there were more than twelve federal firearm-control laws. In 1927, Congress enacted a bill prohibiting small firearms from being mailed to purchasers across state lines. Also during that period, a national conference of state officials proposed the Uniform Firearms Act, directed at handgun control, which was adopted by twenty states during the following decade. The provisions included license requirements, a forty-eight-hour waiting period to purchase a gun, and handgun registration.

TYPES OF GUNS

There are three main categories of guns. Handguns, which are made to be held in one hand, include pistols, derringers, and revolvers. The "long gun" category includes rifles and shotguns. A rifle is usually propped up on one shoulder. It has grooves, called rifling, inside the gun barrel to help the bullet fly straight. A shotgun barrel is not rifled and when fired sends out many little pellets, called shot, at once. The third category consists of guns that must be set on the ground or in a mounting device, such as large machine guns, anti-aircraft guns, and cannons.

Ammunition can be loaded into guns in several different ways. Some guns are loaded one or two bullets at a time, as is done in small derringers or pump-action or bolt-action rifles and shotguns. In guns that are **automatic** or **semiautomatic**, the individual **rounds** of ammunition, called cartridges, are loaded into a container called a **magazine**, or clip, and then placed in the handle of the gun. The magazine of a revolver is a small cylinder that holds usually six cartridges and rotates to load a single cartridge each time the trigger is pulled. Most handguns, however, are automatic or semiautomatic. Some automatic and semiautomatic magazines can hold dozens of cartridges, while handgun magazines generally hold between five and twenty. A semiautomatic gun shoots a cartridge each time the trigger is pulled. The force of the firing ejects the empty bullet casing and inserts the next cartridge into the firing chamber of the gun. A fully automatic gun is one that fires cartridges in rapid succession as long as the trigger is held down. Most fully automatic guns are rifles; some are called machine guns.

Examples of a variety of guns, including pistols, revolvers, shotguns, and automatic weapons.

In 1932, Franklin D. Roosevelt was elected president. When he took office the following year, his inclination was to respond to all the nation's ills with federal legislation. People in rural communities usually owned weapons in order to hunt game or protect themselves from animal predators or petty thugs. People in urban areas, on the other hand, feared an escalation in violent organized crime. It was the time known as the Gangster Era, when notorious mobsters such as Machine Gun Kelly, John Dillinger, and Al Capone, armed with automatic weapons, terrorized, if not the whole nation, the whole nation's psyche. The federal government stepped in and passed the 1934 National Firearms Act (NFA), which sought to rid the nation of automatic weapons, machine guns, automatic rifles, short-barreled shotguns and rifles, and gun silencers. The law also placed a $200 tax on each gun manufactured.

The law was amended in the 1938 Federal Firearms Act to impose more restrictions on selling and shipping firearms. Sellers needed to receive a license and record the names and addresses of every buyer. These restrictions on interstate commerce in firearms were not exclusive to automatic weapons but also covered most handguns and ammunition. The law also forbade selling a gun to anyone with a history of criminal behavior, alcoholism, mental incapacity, or drug abuse.

On November 22, 1963, President John F. Kennedy was assassinated in Dallas, Texas. His killer used a mail-order military-grade sniper rifle. He had paid $19.95 for it. At the time, a Connecticut senator had been pushing for a stricter firearms bill. After the assassination, there were calls for more gun control, but there was no consensus. It was

A federal firearms agent inspects a cache of guns owned by the mobster John Dillinger.

Passengers on a train read the shocking news that President John F. Kennedy was assassinated by gunman Lee Harvey Oswald.

an era of great upheaval in American society. There was the unpopular Vietnam War. Race-based riots were erupting in major cities. In 1968, the civil rights leader Dr. Martin Luther King Jr. and the presidential candidate and brother of President Kennedy, Senator Robert Kennedy, were assassinated. President Lyndon Johnson argued before Congress to pass a bill he called the Safe Streets and Crime Control Act. Arguments for and against the bill were largely divided between citizens of rural areas and urban dwellers. Gun-rights advocates were afraid that hunters, sportsmen, and sportswomen would lose their rights to own guns. They also said that restricting mail-order sales of guns would not

UNITED STATES V. MILLER

The first Supreme Court decision to address the legality of the Second Amendment came in a 1939 case known as *United States v. Miller*. Both gun-rights and gun-control advocates say that the decision supports their position.

On April 18, 1938, two small-time bank robbers and **moonshiners** crossed state lines between Claremont, Oklahoma, and Siloam Springs, Arkansas. The men, Jack Miller and Frank Layton, were caught by federal agents and charged with violating the National Firearms Act—their crime being that they had transported a double-barreled, sawed-off shotgun across state lines and had failed to pay the $200 tax that the NFA levied on automatic weapons and short-barreled shotguns and rifles. At trial in district court in Arkansas, Miller and Layton contended that the NFA was unconstitutional and denied them their Second Amendment right to keep and bear arms. The judge agreed and dismissed the case.

However, the case was appealed by the government to the U.S. Supreme Court. On March 30, 1939, the Supreme Court overturned the Arkansas judge's ruling and declared that the NFA did not violate the Second Amendment. The Court majority opinion stated,

> In the absence of any evidence tending to show that possession or use of a "shotgun having a barrel of less than eighteen inches in length" at this time has some reasonable relationship to the preservation or efficiency of a well regulated militia, we cannot say that the Second Amendment guarantees the right to keep and bear such an instrument. Certainly it is not within judicial notice that this weapon is any part of the ordinary military equipment or that its use could contribute to the common defense.

Both sides of the gun-control/gun-rights debate declared a victory in this decision. Gun-control advocates point out that the Supreme Court interpreted the Second Amendment to mean that the right to own a firearm was protected only in order to maintain a state militia. Gun-rights advocates respond to the decision by saying that the Supreme Court ruled that ownership of a firearm that could be suitable for use in a militia is a protected Second Amendment right.

have prevented the assassinations of Senator Kennedy and Dr. King. Gun-control proponents wanted more regulation, licensing, and limitations on who could own a gun. Both sides compromised on the final bill, the Gun Control Act of 1968. The act prohibited interstate traffic in firearms and ammunition and denied gun ownership to minors, fugitives, drug users, the mentally ill, and persons who had committed a felony. Gun-rights advocates succeeded in preventing mandatory owners' permits and national registration, and gun-control advocates succeeded in outlawing mail-order rifles and shotguns and selling guns to out-of-state purchasers.

In 1972 the Bureau of Alcohol, Tobacco, and Firearms (ATF) was created to enforce the Gun Control Act. The next federal gun-control legislation was in 1986, the Law Enforcement Officers Protection Act, which made it illegal to manufacture or import "cop-killer bullets," that is, ammunition that could pierce bulletproof clothing, such as that worn by police. The Firearms Owners' Protection Act of 1987 lessened restrictions imposed by the 1968 gun-control laws. Out-of-state sales of ammunition, rifles, and shotguns were again allowed, as there was no evidence that the law had any effect on crime. The act also allowed persons to transport their guns across state lines, even when the local laws did not have that provision. Travelers had to carry their firearms "unloaded and inaccessible," meaning that guns and ammunition supplies had to be stored either in the trunk of a car or in a locked box in a vehicle without a trunk. Some restrictions on gun sellers were lifted, and harsher penalties were added for persons who used firearms in

A Washington, D.C., police officer displays a "cop-killer" bullet.

the course of a crime. In 1990, Congress passed the Crime Control Act, which outlawed possession of a gun in a school zone as well as outlawing homemade semiautomatic rifles and shotguns made from legally imported parts.

On November 30, 1993, twelve years after an assassination attempt on President Ronald Reagan, the Brady Handgun Violence Prevention Act was signed into law. On March 30, 1981, a man named John Hinkley stood in a crowd of people outside a Washington, D.C., hotel waiting for President Reagan to appear. When the president turned to wave to the crowd, Hinkley shot six rounds of ammunition from

a .22-**caliber** revolver, strik-
ing the president, an aide,
a police officer, and the
president's press secretary,
James Brady. All recovered,

though Brady, who was shot in the forehead, was left partially para-
lyzed and blind. The Brady Handgun Violence Prevention Act imposed
a five-day waiting period and a background check on any unlicensed
individual before the purchase of a handgun could be made. The act
also required a federal background check system, called the **National
Instant Criminal Background Check System (NICS)**, run by the FBI.
The NICS system could provide an almost immediate response, elec-
tronically or by telephone, so that once it was in place, the five-day
waiting period was no longer required. During the 1980s through the
1990s, violent crime rates were high. A national poll showed that more
than 80 percent of Americans viewed crime as their biggest worry. In
1994, the Violent Crime Control and Law Enforcement Act was signed
into law by President Bill Clinton. It was the largest anticrime bill in the
history of the country. While dealing with many aspects of crime control and prevention, one large part of the bill was the Public Safety and
Recreational Firearms Use Protection Act, which came to be known
as the Assault Weapons Ban. Although more than six hundred handguns, rifles, and shotguns were exempt from the ban, the ban sought
to control nineteen specific semiautomatic weapons, including grenade launchers and gun cartridges that held more than ten rounds of

James Brady looks on as President William J. Clinton signs the anticrime legislation that is often referred to as the "Brady bill."

DID YOU KNOW?

The times have changed: In 1972, U.S. Supreme Court Chief Justice William Rehnquist declared, "The Second Amendment, as noted, was designed to keep alive the militia." In 2010, Supreme Court Justice Samuel Alito stated, "The individual [has the] right to possess and carry weapons in case of confrontation."

ammunition. Though many Americans wanted the government to take action against violent crime, gun-rights advocates were concerned that the antigun legislation would threaten their Second Amendment rights. Legislators on both sides of the debate agreed to a compromise that stated that the ban would expire in 2004, unless a future Congress chose to renew it.

Congress allowed the assault-weapons ban to expire in 2004, and as of 2013, no new federal gun-control measures had been passed.

WHAT DO YOU THINK?

If the Second Amendment refers only to a well regulated militia, why does it include the words "the right of the people"? Why would it not say "Militias have the right to maintain arms"?

On the other hand, if the Second Amendment meant to confer a right to bear arms to individuals, why does the amendment begin "A well regulated militia"?

Do you think the language in the Constitution is absolute? Or do you think that the Constitution can and should be interpreted to reflect changes in society? How does your opinion relate to the Second Amendment?

Do you think the omission of mentioning self-defense in the wording of the Second Amendment is important? Do you agree with the Supreme Court's opinion that there is an "inherent" right to individual gun ownership in the Second Amendment?

Do you believe states and local communities have the right to ban handguns?

Chapter 2

Americans have been gun owners since they settled the colonies. They used their guns for shooting game and for protection against wild animals, invaders, and thieves. They also owned guns to protect themselves from the French and the British armies, enemy Native American tribes, and even the American federal government. America, less than 150 years ago, was a frontier nation. Gun ownership is an American tradition.

Today the estimated 90 million gun owners in the United States own them for a variety of reasons. Twenty million use guns for hunting. In rural or wilderness areas, many people carry guns for protection from bears, wolves, alligators, poisonous snakes, and other animal predators. Besides the sport of hunting, gun owners also participate in the sport of target shooting. Target shooting has been an Olympic competitive event since 1896. According to the National Shooting Sports Foundation, there are 19 million target shooters who participate in safe handgun, rifle, and shotgun sports. Some gun owners are collectors who admire guns for their craftsmanship. They collect them for rarity of manufacture, age, and historical significance. Lastly, many people own guns to protect themselves from crime. Forty-six percent of gun owners say that they own a gun to use for self-defense or to intimidate and deter a criminal.

Hunting wild game is a shooting sport enjoyed by many Americans.

Olympic target shooters compete in the 2008 Olympic Games, held in Beijing, China.

The Framers of the Constitution created a government whose power ultimately derives from the people; having the individual right to own a firearm is an expression of that belief. The Second Amendment Foundation (SAF), an education and legal-rights organization based in Washington State, compares the right of individuals to keep and bear arms to other rights in the Bill of Rights, such as freedom of speech and freedom of religion. Sandra Froman, former president of the National Rifle Association (NRA), wrote, "The right of self-defense is fundamental, and has been recognized in law for centuries." In 1895, for example, the Supreme Court ruled that a citizen "may repel force by force" in self-defense and is "entitled to stand his ground and meet any attack made

> ## DID YOU KNOW?
> The National Rifle Association, founded in 1871, is America's oldest civil rights organization—thirty-eight years older than the National Association for the Advancement of Colored People, and fifty-nine years older than the American Civil Liberties Union.

upon him with a deadly weapon... as needed to prevent great bodily injury or death." The Gun Control Act of 1968 and the Firearm Owners' Protection Act clearly state that people have the right to own guns for "protective purposes."

Responsibility

Most gun owners are responsible, law-abiding citizens. They believe in handling guns safely, being trained to use guns appropriately, and following the law, however much they may disagree with gun-control laws. There are many gun-rights organizations whose members are active in responsible gun ownership. Hunters, for example, follow many gun regulations. They are required to purchase a permit to hunt specific animals at specific times of the year in specific locations, as well as on certain days of the week. Hunters are stewards of the land and are often the largest donors to conservation efforts. They recognize that various hunting rules protect animals when they are breeding or caring for their young. They also understand that the regulations protect other hunters from accidental injury and guard the privacy of property owners. Target shooters practice in controlled environments, such as

Hunting regulations ensure the safety of citizens and protect the environment and wildlife.

shooting ranges, and dedicate themselves to increasing the speed and accuracy of their aim. Many people purchase guns for self-defense and crime prevention. It is entirely in their best interest to know how to care for their guns and how to use them correctly.

Guns and Crime

Americans believe in their right to life, liberty, and happiness, and many people believe guns can help ensure and enable those pursuits. Yet the reality is that there are people with guns who will use them to threaten, steal, abuse, injure, attack, or murder. Many citizens believe owning a gun is their most important means of protection. In 1997, the Australian government required all gun owners to surrender their guns. After more than 640,000 guns were destroyed, crime sta-tistics rose markedly. Aus-

tralians saw that after one year without their firearms, the murder rate rose 6.2 percent, violent assaults with weapons were up 9 percent, and armed robberies rose an astounding 44 percent. As one police officer declared, "Guns in the hands of honest citizens save lives and prop-erty and, yes, gun-control laws only affect the law-abiding citizens." Gun-rights organizations in the United States emphatically say that the police officer's statement is on the mark. Private citizens who own handguns and know how to use them are effective in dispelling violent gun attacks made against them by criminals. In 1986, the city of Chicago banned all handguns. Until the ban was legally challenged before the Supreme Court, the number of murders committed with handguns was about 40 percent higher than before the law took effect. In overturning the ban, Supreme Court Justice Samuel Alito wrote that "Chicago resi-dents now face one of the highest murder rates in the country."

The NRA's Sandra Froman says that crime declines in states with right-to-carry laws. Since Florida adopted right-to-carry laws in 1987, the state's total violent crime dropped 32 percent and its murder rate dropped 58 percent. After Texas established a right-to-carry law in 1996, the violent crime rate dropped 20 percent and the murder rate 31 percent.

GUN-PERMIT PROCEDURES AND POLICIES

State and local governments develop their own gun-permit procedures and policies. (The ATF does not issue firearm permits, except to machine gun owners who possess machine guns manufactured before the Firearms Owners' Protection Act went into effect in 1986.) In most states, a permit is not needed to own a rifle or a shotgun. However, most states and local governments require a permit to own or transport a handgun. The following are various permit policies:

May Issue

A few state and local jurisdictions have a "may issue" policy, which means that a person must have a permit to own a handgun. Applicants must have a clean background check, be a legal resident, and meet age requirements. Other requirements may include submitting fingerprints or a DNA sample and passing a safety-training class. In some may-issue regulations, a gun-permit applicant may be required to justify owning a handgun; people who routinely carry valuables or cash in their line of work (jewelers, shopkeepers, and security guards) are typical applicants. Once the criteria are met, the authorities, such as the state police, sheriff's office, or police department, may elect to issue a permit or deny one at their own discretion. They also have the authority to revoke a permit.

Shall Issue

A "shall issue" jurisdiction (sometimes called "must issue") requires that a person obtain a permit to own a handgun. Once the applicant has met the defined criteria, a handgun permit must be issued.

Qualified or Unlimited Permit

Some states and local governments issue two types of permits. A qualified permit gives permission for a gun owner to carry a gun for sporting-only purposes—hunting or target practice. An unlimited permit grants the permit holder the right to carry a gun for self-defense and defense of personal property.

No Issue

"No issue" jurisdictions do not issue any concealed-weapon permits.

Concealed-Carry / Concealed-Weapon Permit

Most states allow a person to have a long gun or a handgun in the home or place of business, but to carry a concealed handgun in public, governments require a concealed-carry permit.

Open Carry

In areas where concealed-carry laws are restrictive, some gun owners carry their guns in the open. In many places, sport shooters, such as hunters, often carry their guns in plain sight, but visibly carrying a handgun is often regarded as a political protest of concealed-carry permit laws.

Right to Carry

Nearly all states have turned to "right-to-carry" laws, whereby citizens can apply for a permit and, if eligible, will receive a permit to carry a concealed weapon in public. However, some states, such as California, still allow county and city governments to follow may-issue policies. Some states require no permit at all. As of 2011, those states were Alaska, Arizona, Wyoming, and Vermont.

Constitutional Carry

Constitutional carry, or unrestricted carry, relies on Second Amendment rights to "keep and bear arms" and allows both open and concealed carrying of firearms. The unrestricted-carry policy removes all government involvement in gun ownership, such as background checks and requirements of mandatory safety training. In 2011, four states had constitutional-carry laws; other states had laws pending.

Supporters of the right-to-carry laws use statistics from Britain to illustrate their position. In 1987, the United Kingdom banned all handguns. Soon, felony crimes committed with handguns increased by 40 percent. According to the Center for Problem-Oriented Policing, some 60 percent of all burglaries in the United States occur when no one is home. On the other hand, in the United Kingdom, 56 percent of forced-entry burglaries are committed at night or on weekends, when families typically are home. A cause-and-effect scenario can effectively be drawn. American burglars break in when no one is home for fear of getting shot by a homeowner with a gun, whereas British burglars have no reason to worry that they will be confronted by someone pointing a firearm at them. The Second Amendment Foundation asks, "Is it safe NOT to have a gun in your house?"

Police Protection and Private Gun Ownership

Mike Pence, a Republican congressman from Indiana, stated, "I maintain that firearms in the hands of law-abiding citizens makes communities safer, not less safe." Gun-rights proponents say that it makes no sense to disarm citizens when the criminals are armed. They point out that police departments do not have the budgets or the personnel or even the legal mandate to take preventive measures against crimes. In a *San Francisco Examiner* article, Don Kates Jr., a criminologist, wrote, "Even if all 500,000 American police officers were assigned to patrol, they could not protect 240 million citizens from upwards of 10 million criminals who enjoy the luxury of deciding when and where to strike." Several court decisions have upheld state laws that make police immune from lawsuits stemming from a failure to provide police protection from crime. A California court ruled, "Neither a public entity or a public employee [may be sued] for failure to provide adequate police protection or service, failure to prevent the commission

GUN-FREE ZONES

The Gun Free School Zones Act of 1995 enforced stricter penalties on anyone carrying a handgun within a distance of 1,000 feet (305 m) of a public or private school. Many states also restrict persons with concealed-weapons permits from bringing their guns into bars, restaurants, banks, churches, and government buildings. Some states have already passed measures that allow persons with concealed-weapons permits to carry their weapons into these restricted areas, and several state legislatures have bills pending. Gun-rights proponents cite concerns over people who have concealed-weapons permits but because guns are not allowed in certain places or areas, they are forced to leave their guns behind in their vehicle.

Many communities are rethinking weapons bans established for public areas such as schools, churches, restaurants, and bars.

of crimes and failure to apprehend criminals." Police are not required to prevent a violent attack; they are only expected to respond. Citizens making an emergency 9-1-1 call have no guarantee that the police will arrive in time. A Washington, D.C., author and attorney named Richard Stevens explained, "First, police cannot and do not protect everyone from crime. Second, the government and the police in most localities owe no legal duty to protect individuals from criminal attack. When it comes to deterring crime and defending against criminals, individuals are ultimately responsible for themselves and their loved ones. Depending solely on police emergency response means relying on the telephone as the only defensive tool. Too often, citizens in trouble dial 9-1-1... and die."

Gun-rights advocates march in front of the Washington Monument to protest stricter gun-control laws.

Schools and Guns

"A lot of people hear about guns and schools and become alarmed," says David Burnett, a spokesman for a guns-on-campus group named Students for Concealed Carry. As instances of violence on college campuses increase, many students feel that they should have a means to protect themselves. There is an increasing number of students on campus, especially female students, who become victims of violent assault, robbery, rape, and even murder. On April 16, 2007, a disturbed student named Seung-Hui Cho went on a rampage on the campus of the Virginia Polytechnic Institute and, using an automatic handgun, murdered thirty-two people and injured twenty-five more. A year after the Virginia Tech shooting, there were 3,000 sexual assaults, 4,500 robberies, and 5,000 violent attacks on college campuses. Ironically, Virginia Tech was founded as a military academy. Some students there have concealed-weapons permits but are not allowed to bring a gun on campus. Says Burnett, "Stickers on the doors saying 'no guns allowed' won't keep an armed killer out of the building." Students with concealed-carry permits have already gone through a background check and a safety-training class and have possibly been in the military and otherwise have met all other requirements proving they are responsible individuals who can conduct themselves effectively in a crisis. Students for Concealed Carry say that students with concealed-carry permits have the legal right to bring their guns with them anywhere else, but if they "walk onto a college campus, their right to self-defense is taken away."

Women and Guns

Handguns are often the "great equalizers" when it comes to victims and crime. This is especially true for women. The organization Women against Gun Control says, "An increasing number of women are concluding that, when it comes to an encounter with an attacker, 'Guns are a girl's best friend.' Guns give women a fighting chance. Whether a woman is physically fit or not, a gun is the one thing that can equal a man's strength." What should women do if confronted by an attacker? "Should they run? Scream? Call for help? Wrestle the attacker to the ground?" None of these options, the organization says, is as effective as carrying a handgun and knowing how to use it. The group Arming Women against Rape and Endangerment (AWARE) lists the most common threats women victims face: rape, carjacking, purse snatching, stalking, domestic violence, and attacks on their children. Women report more than 94,000 crimes of sexual assault or rape every year, and an unknown number of sexual assault crimes go unreported. A self-defense expert, Bryan Hough, writes that approximately six out of every one hundred women in the United States will become a victim of rape or sexual assault. According to the U.S. Bureau of Justice Statistics, burglaries that take place while someone is in the home, is highest among single women with children. Lyn Bates, the editor of *Women & Guns* magazine, esti-

DID YOU KNOW?

Felony carjacking is a growing crime mainly because most cars on the road now have good antitheft systems. Car thieves know that it is easier to steal a car with a person in it than to steal a locked car from a parking space.

An increasing number of women are choosing to carry handguns for protection.

mates that 1.4 million persons are stalked each year, most of them women. A stalker will telephone, harass, send unwanted mail and e-mail to spy on and track the victim. In a physical attack, a stalker relies on surprise. Bates addresses women in such a threatening situation, "The gun in your hand will be a tremendous comfort, though, because you will know that, if things change to personal assault, you will prevail. Imagine yourself in that situation without a gun. That vulnerability is pretty awful, isn't it, even if you get out unharmed?"

WHY GUN-CONTROL LAWS DON'T WORK

Gun Shows. Department of Justice statistics show that less than one percent of guns used in crimes were purchased at gun shows.

Straw Purchasers. It is punishable up to ten years in prison for a **federal firearms license (FFL)** dealer or a private seller to sell or transfer a firearm or ammunition to someone while knowing or having "reasonable cause to believe" that the person is a prohibited individual. The problem is that a criminal or other prohibited person who wants a gun gets it from a friend, a family member, or on the street and does not care what penalties may befall the dealer, seller, or other transferrer.

Gun-Control Laws. There are more than 25,000 local, state, and federal laws regulating firearm ownership, carry, and transfer. Why then is the United States not the safest country in the world? According to gun-rights proponents, the answer is that criminals do not care about the law; they are by nature lawbreakers. Only law-abiding citizens and upstanding gun dealers obey the laws. The requirements imposed on dealers, sellers, and gun owners are an unnecessary burden. Criminals rarely step up to buy their guns from legitimate sellers because they would fail the background checks. A report of the effectiveness of the NICS background checks prepared by the Department of Justice stated that from November 1998 to December 2008, about 96 million background checks were processed and only 0.007 percent were denied. Given those numbers, gun-rights proponents believe that money could be better spent prosecuting criminals.

Stricter Enforcement. Many gun-rights organizations say that no new gun-control laws are needed, but rather the ones that are in place need to be more strictly enforced. They suggest greater penalties, civil fines, and prison terms for crimes that are committed with guns and stronger penalties still for crimes committed with stolen or prohibited weapons, such as machine guns. Gun-rights organizations want legislators to focus on crime-control efforts that are directed at the felon and the felon's illegal access to firearms and not at firearms themselves or the people who own them legally.

The NRA provides classes and distributes information about gun safety and responsible gun ownership.

Safety

The Second Amendment Foundation says, "One of the fundamental aspects of gun safety is the principle that a gun is a tool, not a toy." Gun safety and training not only reduces the number of accidents, it also ensures that a trained person using a gun in a crisis situation will be effective in fending off an attacker. In 1903, the NRA established rifle clubs at major universities, colleges, and military academies. Since that time, the NRA has been training youths in sports shooting and has been holding sport-shooting competitions. Its members promote safe-sports-shooting programs for other youth groups, such as 4-H clubs, the Boy Scouts of America, and the U.S. Jaycees. In 1988, the NRA established the Eddie Eagle Gun Safety Program. More than 21 million elementary-school children have attended the program and learned about firearm safety. They are taught that when they see a gun and no responsible adult is present, they should "STOP. DON'T TOUCH. LEAVE THE AREA. TELL AN ADULT." The NRA also sponsors a safety program for adults called "Refuse to Be a Victim." The program helps adults form a personal safety plan, which may in part include a firearm. The NRA and other gun-rights organizations provide hundreds of training opportunities for adults and youth. They educate beginner gun owners on buying and loading ammunition, how to shoot with accuracy and speed, how to clean a gun, and suitable ways to store a gun. Owning a gun has responsibilities, but it is a constitutional right.

WHAT DO YOU THINK?

Do you think passing a training class should be mandatory before receiving a handgun permit?

How do you feel about people carrying concealed guns in places that serve alcohol?

Do you think the outcome would have been different and more lives saved if the Virginia Tech students who had concealed-weapons permits had been allowed to carry their weapons on campus?

Do you think the Constitutional Carry movement best reflects the meaning of the Second Amendment?

Chapter 3

"**Firearms** are used to kill two out of every three **homicide** victims in America," says a study published by the Harvard Injury Control Research Center. In examining the relationship between household firearm ownership and rates of homicide, researchers found that homicide rates are higher in states where more households have guns. "One thing is certain," writes Pamela Hartigan in the *Encyclopedia of Public Health*, "The more guns there are in circulation, the greater the likelihood that they will be misused."

There is a mounting concern among gun-control advocates over the number of crimes in which guns, particularly high-caliber weapons, are used. They say there are three major ways guns are damaging society: easy access to guns and high-caliber ammunition, numerous legal loopholes, and a lack of support for law enforcement. Georges C. Benjamin, the executive director of the American Public Health Association (APHA), stated, "Gun violence is a major public health problem that needs to be addressed through a variety of actions, including legislation and regulation."

A Glock semiautomatic handgun was left behind at this crime scene.

Ease of Access

The United States ranks first in the world in private gun ownership. An estimated 280 million guns in the United

States are owned by about 90 million people in a population of approximately 300 million. Gun-control advocates point out that there are nearly as many guns as people in this country, a fact that makes it the most heavily armed country in the world. The United States ranks

Many Americans purchase their guns at gun shows. Laws vary widely from state to state.

THE TIAHRT AMENDMENTS

The Tiahrt Amendments are laws tacked on to federal spending bills originally sponsored by Todd Tiahrt, a Republican congressman from Kansas. The first amendments were added to legislation in 2003 and were intended to maintain confidentiality for gun owners and dealers, but the outcome has prevented law enforcement officers from being as effective as they could be in prosecuting criminals who use and deal in guns. Some of the earlier provisions have been eased, but those still in effect include the following:

NICS background check data is destroyed after twenty-four hours.

This provision makes it difficult to track, find, and prosecute gun dealers who break the law and to identify "straw" purchasers (people who buy guns for others who could not pass a background check).

Prevent ATF from requiring that gun dealers perform an annual inventory to see if and how many firearms are lost or stolen.

Many illegally traded guns are originally stolen or go "missing" from gun retailers.

State and local authorities are limited in using ATF trace data to investigate corrupt gun dealers and patterns of gun traffickers.

Trace data includes information on where guns recovered from crimes were originally purchased. The fact that trace data can also show how soon those guns are used in out-of-state crimes helps law enforcement officers recognize patterns of illegal gun trafficking.

Not until 2010 did law enforcement officials gain access to some of the trace data. State and local police are still not allowed to use the data to prosecute gun dealers who break the law.

fourth in the world in violent crime, after South Africa, Colombia, and Thailand. According to the ATF, there are approximately 4.5 million new firearms sold each year, including about 2 million handguns, as well as another 2 million firearms sold secondhand by private parties.

The Gun-Show Loophole

In 2009, law enforcement officers conducting an undercover sting operation at gun shows in Ohio, Tennessee, and Nevada found that 63 percent of private sellers sold to purchasers who could not pass a background check. Ninety-four percent of licensed dealers at the shows had sold to criminals and "straw purchasers"—gun buyers who say they are making their purchase for private use but are actually buying guns for criminals, minors, domestic-violence offenders, and any other person unable to purchase a gun legally.

On display are the weapons Dylan Klebold and Eric Harris used in their murderous rampage at Columbine High School.

A BROTHER SPEAKS OUT

A chilling example of how simple it is to obtain a handgun is described in an account by a young man whose sister was murdered in the largest school massacre in the United States, the 2007 Virginia Tech shooting. Two years later, the victim's brother went to a Virginia gun show with $5,000 in cash and a plan to see how many guns he could purchase in one hour. Standing outside the gun show, waiting in line to go in, he was approached by a gun seller who offered him a Glock pistol, the same kind as that used to kill his sister. The brother later described the transaction to ABC News.

"How much do you want for it?"

The seller replied, "Four hundred fifty bucks."

"Here's the cash."

"Thanks. See you later." The seller walked away.

"That was it," the brother said afterward.

After his original purchase, the young man entered the gun show and in one hour purchased ten guns. He was never asked to fill out a background check, and in one instance when a seller requested identification, the brother said he had none and was still allowed to purchase two guns for an extra $100. Said the brother, "I got two guns for $600 without any identification check. Anybody can do it. It's that easy. Anyone."

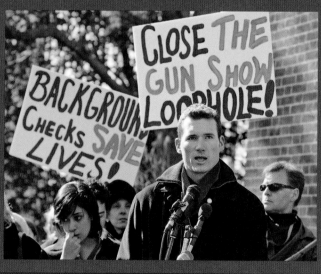

On April 20, 1999, in Littleton, Colorado, two students from Columbine High School, Eric Harris and Dylan Klebold, opened fire on their classmates and teachers; twelve students and one teacher were killed and twenty-one others injured. A straw purchaser, who had not been asked to undergo a background check when she made her purchase from an unlicensed gun seller, supplied the boys with two shotguns, an assault rifle, and a TEC-9 assault pistol. The boys themselves were able to buy the bullets they used in the massacre from a Kmart store in town.

Gun-control advocates see the lack of regulation at gun shows as the most dangerous factor leading to gun-related crime. There are two ways guns are sold in the United States—through licensed sellers and unlicensed private sellers. A licensed seller must have a federal firearms license (FFL) and must perform a background check using the National Instant Background Check System (NICS) to be certain that the buyer is not a criminal, a domestic-violence offender, mentally unstable, or any other type of prohibited purchaser. FFL sellers also must keep records of their sales so that if a gun is used in a crime and is recovered by police, the police can trace the gun back to the buyer. Unlicensed sellers, usually hobbyists or gun collectors, are considered **occasional sellers**. There are no clear guidelines to help define an occasional seller, and many gun-control advocates suspect that there

DID YOU KNOW?

According to a report by the U.S. Police Foundation, no-check gun sales account for 40 percent of gun purchases each year.

are numerous sellers who circumvent the law by calling themselves occasional sellers but who are in fact unlicensed gun dealers. Occasional sellers are not required to keep records of their sales or to run background checks on their customers. At issue are the more than four thousand gun shows held around the country each year. Both licensed and unlicensed sellers participate, as well as gun sellers who have lost their licenses. Show promoters rarely do background checks on sellers. Many licensed gun dealers caution against purchasing from the occasional sellers, but gun shows are full of occasional sellers. Because the sellers congregate at gun shows, felons and other prohibited persons can find them easily and take advantage of unregulated purchases. Gun show regulations vary state by state. Most shows do not require mandatory background checks for buyers. Some states call for gun show promoters to require that gun sellers do background checks and keep records of sales, but many do not. Thirty-three states have no laws requiring background checks at gun shows. Only a few states require checks on all firearm sales, and just three require them on handgun sales. Seven other states require that buyers at gun shows undergo a background check and obtain a permit before making a firearm purchase. That requirement has a serious flaw, though, in that persons who have received a permit can later perpetrate a prohibited activity without having the permit affected or revoked.

In March 2010, John Patrick Bedell, a computer engineer from California with a history of mental illness, attempted to buy a gun from a local dealer. He failed to pass the California state background

An occasional seller advertises no-background-check gun sales before a Colorado law goes into effect requiring all sellers to perform background checks.

check, the strictest in the nation. However, nineteen days later, the man bought a 9 mm Ruger handgun from a private seller at a Las Vegas gun show without going through a background check. After his purchase, he drove to the Pentagon in Washington, D.C., and shot two Pentagon police officers. Commenting on the assault, a Los Angeles county sheriff admitted that "[the] key is anyone can leave California and buy a gun anywhere else that doesn't have strong gun laws. Whether you're mentally ill or stable, either way, guns are easily accessible because states have different policies." For this reason, say gun-control advocates, a national law closing the gun show loophole is necessary.

On July 20, 2012, in Aurora, Colorado, a gunman opened fire on a crowd in a movie theater. One of the deadliest mass shootings in U.S. history, the horrific incident took place during a midnight showing of *The Dark Knight Rises*. The shooter, James Eagan Holmes, was heavily armed, dressed in protective gear, and wearing a gas mask. He fired on the unsuspecting crowd, killing 12 and injuring 58 more individuals.

Among his trove of weapons in the theater was a shotgun, a semi-automatic rifle, and handguns; the police found more firearms behind the cinema and in the killer's vehicle.

Then, on December 14—just over five months after Aurora—at the Sandy Hook elementary school in Newtown, Connecticut, a young man named Adam Lanza shot his way into the school as the regular classes began. Brandishing a gun and hundreds of rounds of ammunition, he killed 26 individuals. Six were adults, and the remaining twenty were children, all between the ages of six and seven. Lanza had shot and killed his mother earlier in the day. This tragedy was the second deadliest in U.S. history, after Virginia Tech just five years earlier.

The December 2012 shooting in Newtown, Connecticut was devastating to the families of the victims and the community at large.

State Recordkeeping

Gun-control advocates say the NICS system has other shortcomings that need to be addressed. Mental health is one such issue. Federal law disqualifies individuals who are mentally unfit from purchasing guns, yet many states do not provide pertinent information to the NICS database, nor are there federal requirements for states to do so. Because records are incomplete, especially mental-health reports, ineligible persons succeed in acquiring firearms. Such was the case with the Virginia Tech shooter, who had a court order declaring him mentally ill and dangerous, yet because of concerns over privacy issues, the state of Virginia never supplied the information to NICS. The shooter passed the background check and legally purchased the firearms to use in his bloody rampage. The Brady Center states, "Unfortunately, many prohibited persons are not blocked from buying guns because their records are not in the NICS, including about 80 or 90 percent of individuals with disqualifying mental-health records, and one-fourth of those with felony convictions. Ten states do not provide any relevant domestic violence records that indicate prohibited purchasers." Bob Carpenter, a vice president of a Republican polling firm said, "Americans and gun owners feel with equal fervor that government must act to get every single record in the background-check system that belongs there and to ensure that every gun sale includes a background check." The Brady Center and the Violence Policy Center supported the NICS Improvement Amendments Act of 2007 passed by Congress, which

MEXICAN DRUG WARS AND BORDER GUN TRAFFICKING

In 2010, a report from the Government Accountability Office (GAO) found that more than 70 percent of assault weapons and other high-powered firearms confiscated in Mexican drug war violence could be traced back to gun dealers in the southern border states of Texas, Arizona, New Mexico, and California. The ATF wanted to require gun dealers in the border states to report sales of more than two assault weapons and any semiautomatic gun greater than .22 caliber with a detachable magazine. Declaring that the program violated the privacy of assault-weapons buyers, the House of Representatives, with the lobbying support of the NRA, refused to fund the program. According to the *Washington Post*, since 2006 the more than 60,000 U.S. guns recovered in Mexico have contributed to more than 30,000 murders. The vice president of the Prosecuting Attorneys Association, Steven Jansen, said that the ATF was "handcuffed by ineffective and weak laws." He said that straw purchasers supply Mexican drug cartels with U.S. military-style weapons. These activities add to the flow of Mexican drugs into the United States while endangering communities in border states. Dennis Henigan, vice president of the Brady Center to Prevent Gun Violence, said, "The traffickers are going to American gun shops, exploiting the permissive U.S. gun laws. It's beyond time for the United States to strengthen its gun laws and shut down the trafficking."

A display of guns smuggled from the United States that were seized from Mexican drug dealers.

DID YOU KNOW?

The Brady background-check law has prevented nearly 2 million prohibited persons from illegally buying guns.

Individuals who are prohibited from purchasing a firearm include minors and those who have been convicted of or are under indictment for a crime punishable by imprisonment for more than one year, as well as

- fugitives from justice
- unlawful users of a controlled substances or addicts and those who have been adjudicated as mentally defective or are committed to a mental institution
- illegal aliens
- those who have been dishonorably discharged from the military
- those who have renounced U.S. citizenship
- those who are subject to a court order restraining them from harassing, stalking, or threatening intimate partners, their children or children of a partner or engaging in other conduct that would place an intimate partner in reasonable fear of bodily injury to the partner or child
- those who have been convicted of a misdemeanor offense of domestic violence

provides grant money to states to help them supply more thorough records to NICS.

Terrorists

Gun-control advocates fear that terrorism from both domestic and foreign groups is on the rise. After the U.S. military killed Osama bin Laden, the leader of the terrorist group Al Qaeda, an American-born spokesman for the group released a video in which he said, "America is absolutely awash with easily obtainable firearms. You can go down to a gun show at the local convention center and come away with a fully automatic assault rifle without a background check and, most likely, without having to show an identification card. So what are you waiting for?" The more than 400,000 persons on the FBI's terrorist watch list are not prohibited from purchasing a firearm unless they are convicted of a felony or fall under any of the other prohibitions. Said the director of Mayors Against Guns, "A terror suspect can't take a regular sized tube of Crest into the airport, much less board a plane, but they can buy an AK-47 with no questions asked." From 2004 to 2010, 1,228 persons on the terrorist watch list were subjected to a background check before purchasing firearms, and 91 percent of the gun sales were approved. For the safety of American citizens, gun-control advocates believe it is entirely justified to require watch-list information to be added to the NICS database. They also support allowing the Department of Justice the flexibility to deny such individuals from legally purchasing firearms, regardless of whether or not they have committed a crime.

Assault Weapons

The federal assault-weapons ban, as well as a ban on high-capacity ammunition magazines, expired in 2004. Gun-control advocates, and even some gun-rights proponents, want the ban restored and strengthened. A multitude of tragedies have occurred at the hands of shooters who have used high-powered assault weapons to kill innocent victims

and law enforcement officers. On November 5, 2009, an army officer, Major
Nidal Malik Hasan, wielded a semiautomatic pistol (often used by military SWAT
teams) and opened fire at a military hos-
pital in Fort Hood, Texas. In just ten min-
utes, Major Hasan murdered thirteen un-
armed people and wounded thirty-two
others. The gunman had repeatedly visit-
ed a local gun shop, where he purchased
several boxes of armor-piercing "cop
killer" bullets, once illegal for sale under
the assault-weapons ban. Each box con-

Major Nidal Malik Hasan, the doctor who
was responsible for killing 13 people in a
massacre at Fort Hood, Texas, is shown
here in an official Army photograph.

tained fifty bullets and cost $23.99. Although the gunman was filmed
on videotape asking how to use the gun and the ammunition, there
was no law requiring that his purchases be questioned. During his
shooting rampage, he fired off 214 rounds of ammunition and, after
being felled by a civilian policewoman called to the scene, was found
to possess another 177 rounds of unspent ammunition. The policewoman was also shot, but she recovered. Hubert Williams, president
of the Police Foundation, who has supported the assault-weapons ban,
said, "For the nation's police, such weapons present daily and deadly
challenges to their ability to protect the public."

The violence continues. On January 8, 2011, in the parking lot of a
Tucson, Arizona, grocery store, Congresswoman Gabrielle Giffords had

set up a table to talk to voters. With her aides and constituents gathered around her, Jared Loughner, a troubled twenty-two-year-old man, opened fire with a high-capacity-magazine, semiautomatic Glock pistol, the same one used by the Virginia Tech gunman. Loughner sent a bullet through the congresswoman's brain and in the next fifteen seconds killed six other people, including a federal judge, a nine-year-old girl, and one of Giffords's aides, and wounded fourteen others. After firing thirty-three rounds, Loughner stopped to reload. At that point, several people in the crowd came forward to wrestle him to the ground.

> **DID YOU KNOW?**
> "It shouldn't be as easy to buy a high-capacity gun magazine at a sporting goods store as it is to purchase a magazine at the corner newsstand."
> —Senator Frank Lautenberg

Only a few states limit the capacity of magazines, and in Arizona, where gun-control laws are some of the least restrictive in the nation, there is no limit on magazine capacity, and no permits are required to carry a concealed weapon. New Jersey senator Frank Lautenberg, long a supporter of an assault-weapons ban, wrote, "These are the kinds of guns soldiers used on faraway battlefields; they don't belong in our communities.... Yet Loughner—despite his past—being kicked out of college and rejected for Army service—legally purchased the guns and ammunition police say he used in the massacre. Our country deemed Loughner unfit to wear its uniform—but it was perfectly legal for him to purchase the lethal weaponry he is accused of using to kill innocent people in a supermarket parking lot." At a press conference about passing a new assault-weapons ban, Ross Zimmerman, the father of Gabe Zimmerman, the murdered congressional aide, asked, "What is so hard about the idea of common sense, responsible behavior; what is so hard about banning something like this?"

Sensible Gun Laws

What are some of the gun-control laws that work? Even in polls of NRA members, many believe that sensible gun-control laws will make people safer. Gun-control advocates believe laws should (1) require gun sellers, licensed and occasional sellers, to conduct NICS background checks on all purchasers; (2) require states to submit court records of persons who have committed crimes, have used or dealt drugs, have restraining orders in place against them, have been involved in domestic violence, and have been declared mentally unfit; (3) prohibit people on the terrorist watch list from purchasing guns; (4) limit gun magazines to ten rounds of ammunition; (5) limit the number of guns, especially handguns, a buyer can purchase within a month; (6) require handgun owners to be licensed; (7) require permits to carry a concealed weapon; (8) prohibit the sale of assault weapons and strengthen the definition of such weapons so that manufacturers cannot circumvent the law; (9) require households with minors to store

DID YOU KNOW?

According to a study reported by the Violence Policy Center, 82 percent of teens who committed suicide with a firearm used one from their home, usually a parent's weapon. During the period when Washington, D.C., was allowed to ban handguns, the city had a lower suicide rate of youth than that of any state.

SAFETY

According to recent statistics compiled by the Brady Campaign to Stop Gun Violence, there is a correlation between the states with the highest number of gun murders and the weakness of their gun laws. Conversely, states with the lowest number of gun murders have some of the strongest gun-control laws. Hawaii, Massachusetts, Connecticut, and New Jersey, which have very restrictive gun laws, are the four states with the lowest murder rates. The states with the least gun restrictions, Alaska, Louisiana, Wyoming, and Arizona, have the highest murder rates per 100,000 residents.

A study published by the *Journal of American Medicine* reported that in households with safely stored guns, there are significantly fewer deaths or injuries to children and teens compared to households where guns are stored loaded or in unlocked containers.

Methods of storing guns safely include locking guns, storing guns in a locked container, and storing ammunition separate from firearms. While many gun owners keep guns for self-defense, reports have shown that people who possess firearms in their homes are forty-three times more likely to kill or injure a family member or friend than an intruder. The position of the American Academy of Pediatrics on gun safety in a home with children is simple: "The safest thing is to not have a gun in your home, especially not a handgun." Yet, in 2011 in Florida, a law was passed prohibiting doctors from asking if there is a gun in the home. NRA spokespeople say that the question is an invasion of privacy. Doctors traditionally ask questions about safety in the home, especially to first-time parents. According to Dr. Louis St. Petery, a Florida pediatric heart surgeon, "It's all part of what doctors call 'anticipatory guidance'—teaching parents how to safeguard against accidental injuries. Pediatricians ask about bike helmets, seat belts, and other concerns. If you have a pool, let's talk about pool safety so we don't have accidental drowning. And if you have firearms, let's talk about gun safety so that they're stored properly—you know, the gun needs to be locked up, the ammunition stored separate from the gun, etcetera so that children don't have access to them."

Police officers hand out gun locks in a community program designed to promote gun safety in the home, especially in households with young children.

guns locked and unloaded; (10) require gun owners to notify law enforcement if a gun is lost or stolen; and (11) enable law enforcement to have full access to NICS trace data.

WHAT DO YOU THINK?

Do you think gun-control laws should be enacted by the federal government? By individual states?

Do you think a person's mental-health records, not just court declarations of incompetence, should be a part of the NICS database?

Persons on the terrorist watch list have not necessarily committed a crime. Do you think that their rights are being abused if those persons' names are submitted to NICS?

If the assault-weapons ban were to be reenacted, how would you make changes to the law?

Ammunition is inexpensive and can be purchased at most sporting goods stores. Would you change or regulate those sales?

Chapter 4

Gun-rights proponents and gun-control proponents can often be apart politically; yet many still find common ground. True, there are those who would ban all guns outright and demand that gun owners surrender their weapons, as was done in Australia and the United Kingdom. Conversely, there are those who feel that there should be no restrictions on types of guns or methods of sale and no government involvement in firearm transactions and ownership. America is a democratic nation whose laws reflect the diversity of the people. Is it possible to reach common ground on gun control and gun rights?

Guns and Self-Defense

Many people would agree that gun owners are largely responsible people who know how to correctly use and care for their weapons. Rarely do gun-control advocates take issue with people who are trained and use their guns for sport—target shooting and hunting. The largest disagreement between gun-control and gun-rights advocates concerns the relation between guns and crime. As stated earlier, the majority of gun owners say that they own a firearm for self-defense from an attack or burglary. Citizens living in urban or high-crime areas often think

A man wears his handgun in a holster in an example of the rights permitted by "open carry" laws.

it essential to carry a gun or to keep a gun at home to protect family and property. Yet there are often-asked questions, "Do private citizens who own guns make communities safer? Does gun ownership lead to higher or lower crime rates? Should there be limits and restrictions to the types of guns and ammunition sold? Do background checks and gun permits invade the privacy of gun owners, or do they help law enforcement in fighting crime?"

Gun-rights advocates cite countless incidents in which a person with a firearm thwarts an attack on the street, prevents a home burglary, or a convenience store clerk who does not have time to call 9-1-1 forces a nighttime robber to flee by pulling a handgun from underneath the counter.

Gun-control advocates say having a weapon and knowing how to use it in an intense and emotional situation is not always possible for an average citizen. "Even police miss," they say. Arnold Grossman, author of *One Nation under Guns*, explains that TV and movie scenes showing standoffs are not reality. "The quickest draw is the winner," he writes. Is every person who carries a gun willing to shoot it? It is important to remember that choosing to use lethal force with a firearm must be done only when lives are at stake. Shooting someone only to protect private property is often against the law. The NRA and other gun-rights groups recognize that owning a firearm is a tremendous responsibility and urge all gun owners to be trained in accuracy and safety. As one former soldier commented, "When you have a gun, especially when it's loaded, you have to think about it all the time."

TUCSON

Arizona has few gun-control laws. Many citizens own firearms and carry handguns. There are no permits required. The shooting of Congresswoman Gabrielle Giffords brought to light how complicated the debate can be between gun-rights and gun-control advocates. First of all, Representative Giffords owned a handgun herself, and in an interview with the *New York Times*, she said, "I have a Glock 9 millimeter, and I'm a pretty good shot." The judge who was shot and killed alongside her was a target shooter, and the surgeon who took the bullet out of her brain was a member of a gun club. Gun-rights proponents believe that if the victims had been carrying their weapons, they could have prevented the catastrophe. The judge would normally have been carrying his gun, but it was a Sunday, and people thought it likely that he had been at church before the incident. He was known as a very good marksman. On the other hand, gun-control proponents, such as the Violence Policy Center, say that it is not likely that either of the victims would have been able to respond quickly enough, nor would it have been safe to fire into a crowd of moving, frightened people. Although the shooter owned the same type of gun as the congresswoman, his had a high-capacity detachable magazine capable of holding thirty rounds of ammunition. It was not until he stopped to reload that people in the crowd tackled him.

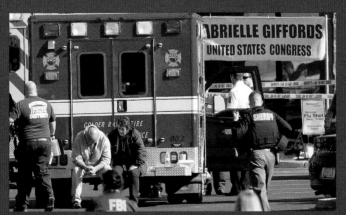

Emergency workers and law enforcement officials work in the Safeway store parking lot in the aftermath of the shooting of Congresswoman Gabrielle Giffords and other victims.

Legislation

"The problem with groups like Mayors against Illegal Guns," says the NRA, "is that they are actually a group that proposes gun-control legislation, which will only affect law-abiding citizens. If you would just do some rudimentary research on existing gun laws and penalties that apply to them, you would find that existing laws are adequate." Gun-control advocates say that everyone should be required to have a license to purchase or sell a gun. They also believe that safety-training classes, like those required to own a handgun in Canada, should be mandatory before a gun permit is issued. Taking a safety test before a gun permit is issued, they believe, is no different from taking a driver's license test before receiving a driver's license. The government licenses cars, boats, and airplanes; why not guns? Gun-rights groups retort that owning a car, boat, or airplane is not a constitutional right. Not only do gun-rights groups provide safe-

Police inspectors try to recover the serial number of an altered handgun used in a crime.

DID YOU KNOW?

Each firearm sold is required by law to have a serial number, a unique identifying mark. Many guns found at crime scenes have had the serial number scratched out.

ty training and marksmanship classes, but most legitimate gun owners come from families of gun owners who teach their children how to use guns carefully and with respect.

"If you outlaw guns, then only outlaws will have guns" is an often-cited adage of gun-rights groups. Gun-rights groups say that by banning guns or making guns more difficult to purchase legally, criminals will simply smuggle guns into the country or make them. Gun-control groups argue that most of the gun sales in the United States were originally legal but then through gun shows, straw purchasers, thefts, and unscrupulous gun dealers, guns make their way into the black market for sale to criminals. If there are fewer legal guns in circulation, say gun-control advocates, then there will be fewer illegal guns in the hands of criminals. Everyone acknowledges that criminals are not going to be deterred by gun laws, but background checks and permits make it more difficult for a criminal to walk into a corner gun shop and purchase a gun outright. Because of the variations in state laws, criminals can purchase guns in regions where laws are less restrictive. Gun-rights advocates say that gun-control laws will not prevent criminals from getting guns; rather, they take guns away from law-abiding citizens and thus deny them their constitutional right to self-defense.

National Instant Criminal Background Check System (NICS)

On average, 211 persons a day are turned away at gun stores, according to the Brady Center. However, the information provided by the states and the FBI is incomplete. In addition to convictions that are not posted, the records of drug users, mentally unfit persons, and persons convicted of domestic violence are often not provided to the NICS database. Officials say that there are millions of boxes of criminal records languishing in courthouse basements, and there is not the technology or funding to submit these records to NICS. Gun-rights groups say that the NICS system only makes it difficult for law-abiding citizens to obtain a permit; criminals do not go through the system. According to the Center for Public Integrity, the largest loophole in the NICS system is the lack of accurate information about persons with histories of domestic violence, drug use, or mental illness. Given that many such prohibited persons lie to obtain a permit and buy a gun, the government wants access to state records of all gun-permit holders. Law enforcement groups feel that access to the permits database would help track criminals as well as prohibited persons who have slipped through the cracks of state databases. Access to state gun-permit records would also uncover where guns used in crimes were purchased. Gun-rights proponents give that idea an emphatic "no." It is an invasion of the privacy of legal gun owners, they say.

Gun-control proponents say that gun-control laws curtail sales to criminals and other prohibited persons. Federal laws regarding background checks, permits, gun shows, and up-to-date police and mental-health records help reduce crime. Moreover, gun-control groups insist that gun-control laws do not infringe on the constitutional right to bear arms. Gun-rights proponents say that gun-control laws are not effective

BACKGROUND CHECKS
$10.00 PER CALL   SALES TAX MUST
TO CBI   BE COLLECTED

NOTICE
NO ONE MAY TRANSFER
A FIREARM WITHOUT
FIRST OBTAINING A
BACKGROUND CHECK
THROUGH A LICENSED
GUN DEALER IF ANY
PART OF THE
TRANSACTION OCCURS
C_____ PREMISES/OR
_____ FACILITIES.
12-26.1-101

Private gun-show sellers are instructed on how to perform NICS background checks on their customers.

in keeping guns out of the hands of criminals. Gun-control laws serve only to create unnecessary burdens on law-abiding gun owners. Further, gun-rights groups say, the more people carrying firearms, the better the deterrent to crime. John Stossel, a television news reporter, commented, "One nice thing about concealed weapons is that even people who don't carry guns are safer because the muggers can't tell who is armed and who isn't."

A Pew Research Center poll taken in 2010 reported that 60 percent of residents on the East Coast favored gun control while 36 percent supported gun rights. In the Midwest, 52 percent were for gun rights, and 44 percent preferred gun control. The South was split, though the states of Alabama, Kentucky, Mississippi, and Tennessee were 60 percent for

Otis McDonald stands in front of the U.S. Supreme Court building after winning his suit challenging gun-control laws in Chicago.

gun rights. On June 28, 2010, the Supreme Court's ruling in *Chicago v. McDonald* confirmed an individual's right to own firearms as the law of the land. The justices' decision was not unanimous, however; it may reflect the fact that the nation continues to be divided or at least conflicted by gun-control and gun-rights positions. Expressing his opinion on the ruling, President Barack Obama stated, "Today's ruling, the first clear statement on this issue in 127 years, will provide much-needed guidance to local jurisdictions across the country. What works in Chicago may not work in Cheyenne, but the decision reinforced that if we act responsibly, we can both protect the constitutional right to bear arms and keep our communities and our children safe."

WHAT DO YOU THINK?

In 2011, a credit card reform bill was passed by Congress. Tacked on to the bill was an amendment making it legal to carry a concealed weapon in national parks. What do you think this legislation says about the divide America faces on gun control and gun rights?

Do you think law enforcement should have access to names of gun-permit holders?

Given that there are many databases involved in the NICS system, do you think that the three-day deadline for providing a response is reasonable? After three days, if no decision is reached, the permit application is granted by default. Do you think the deadline is fair?

Do you think passing a mandatory firearms-training class should be law?

Timeline

1791—The Bill of Rights, which includes the Second Amendment, is ratified by the thirteen original colonies.

1836—Samuel Colt receives the patent for the Colt revolver.

1865—Several southern states pass gun-control laws restricting the sale of guns to the newly emancipated slaves.

1871—The National Rifle Association (NRA) is formed.

1911—The Sullivan Act is passed, requiring individuals to have a permit to own and carry a pistol.

1927—The Uniform Firearms Act is proposed during a national conference of state officials and directed toward handgun control.

1939—The first Supreme Court decision to address the legality of the Second Amendment is in a case known as *United States v. Miller*.

November 22, 1963—President John F. Kennedy is assassinated in Dallas, Texas.

1968—Civil Rights leader Dr. Martin Luther King and presidential candidate and brother of President Kennedy, Senator Robert Kennedy, are assassinated.

1968—Congress passes the Gun Control Act of 1968, prohibiting interstate traffic in firearms and ammunition, and denying the sale of guns to minors, fugitives, drug users, and felons.

1972—The Bureau of Alcohol, Tobacco, and Firearms (ATF) is created to enforce the Gun Control Act.

March 30, 1981—Hinkley fails in his assassination attempt of President Ronald Reagan but seriously wounds the president's press secretary James Brady.

1993—Named after James Brady, the Brady Handgun Violence Act is signed into law by President Bill Clinton, mandating comprehensive background checks on individuals before selling them guns.

(continued on next page)

Timeline *(continued from previous page)*

1994—The Violent Crime Control and Law Enforcement Act is signed into law by President Bill Clinton, banning nineteen specific semiautomatic weapons, including grenade launchers and gun cartridges that hold more than ten rounds.

April 20 , 1999—Two students from Columbine High School, Eric Harris and Dylan Klebold, open fire on their classmates and teachers, killing thirteen and injuring twenty-one others.

2004—Ten years after it first became law, Congress allows a provision banning possession of magazines holding more than ten rounds of ammunition to expire, though a future Congress may choose to renew it. As of 2013, no new federal gun-control measures have been passed.

2007— The U.S. Court of Appeals for the District of Columbia rules to allow Dick Heller, a licensed D.C. police officer, to keep a handgun in his home in Washington, D.C. Following that ruling, the defendants petition the U.S. Supreme Court to hear the case.

April 16, 2007—Seung-Hui Cho, a student attending Virginia Polytechnic, goes on a shooting rampage and kills thirty-two people and injures twenty-five.

June 2008—The United States Supreme Court upholds the verdict of a lower court, ruling the D.C. handgun ban unconstitutional in the landmark case *District of Columbia v. Heller*.

November 5, 2009—U.S. Army officer Major Nidal Malik Hasan opens fire on a military base in Fort Hood, Texas, murdering thirteen and wounding thirty-two.

June 28, 2010—The U.S. Supreme Court's ruling in *Chicago v. McDonald* confirms an individual's right to own firearms.

January 8, 2011—Jared Loughner opens fire on a group of people gathered outside a Tucson, Arizona, grocery store to listen to Congresswoman Gabrielle Giffords. Using a high-capacity, semiautomatic pistol, Loughner kills six. Fourteen people are injured in the attack, including Congresswoman Giffords.

July 20, 2012—A gunman opened fire on a crowd in a movie theater killing 12 and injuring 58.

December 14, 2012—Adam Lanza shot his way into Sandy Hook Elementary School in Newtown, Connecticut, killing 26 people. Six were adults, and 20 were children. The children were between the ages of six and seven. Lanza had shot and killed his mother earlier in the day.

Glossary

advocate—A person who defends a particular cause.

automatic firearm—A firearm that continues to discharge ammunition as long as the trigger is pulled and held.

caliber—The diameter, expressed as a decimal fraction of an inch, of the inside of the barrel of a gun or the outside of a bullet.

federal firearms license (FFL)—A federally mandated authorization that firearm manufacturers and sellers need to obtain in order to conduct business.

firearms—Any weapon which fires ammunition through the use of gunpowder.

homicide—Murder.

magazine—A device that holds the ammunition to be fed into a firearm; a magazine may be fixed (part of the firearm) or detachable.

militia—A group of armed citizens acting as a military unit.

moonshiner—A person who makes or sells illegal liquor.

National Instant Criminal Background Check System (NICS)—An FBI-managed automated system that checks FBI and state databases for the mental-health, immigration-status, and criminal records of prospective gun purchasers. FFL owners access the system at the time of sale to determine whether the purchaser is permitted to complete the transaction.

occasional seller—A person who sells firearms privately and is thus not subject to the FFL requirements.

revolver—A handgun with a rotating cylinder that usually holds six rounds. Each time the trigger is pulled, a bullet is propelled through the barrel; the fired bullet's casing is then ejected, and the rotating cylinder aligns a new round with the barrel.

round—A bullet.

semiautomatic—A firearm that can be switched either to fire one round at a time or to continue to load ammunition as long as the trigger is held.

Find Out More

Books

Gerdes, Louise I., ed. *Gun Violence*. Farmington Hills, MI: Greenhaven Press, 2011.

Grossman, Arnold. *One Nation under Guns: An Essay on an American Epidemic*. Golden, CO: Fulcrum, 2006.

Milite, George A., *Gun Control*. San Diego: Reference Point Press, 2007.

Sakora, Lea, ed. *Is Gun Ownership a Right?* Farmington Hills, MI: Greenhaven Press, 2010.

Websites

Bureau of Justice Statistics
http://bjs.ojp.usdoj.gov/content/guns.cfm
http://bjs.ojp.usdoj.gov

Common Sense about Kids and Guns
www.kidsandguns.org

Gun Policy
www.gunpolicy.org

Washington Cease Fire
www.washingtonceasefire.org

Organizations

Coalition to Stop Gun Violence

1424 L Street NW, Suite 2-1

Washington, D.C. 20005

202-408-0061

www.csgv.org

Gun Owners of America

8001 Forbes Place, Suite 102

Springfield, VA 22151

703-321-8585

www.gunowners.org

National Shooting Sports Foundation, Inc.

11 Mile Hill Road

Newtown, CT 06470

203-426-1320

www.nssf.org

Second Amendment Foundation

12500 NE 10th Place

Bellevue, WA 98005

425-454-7012

www.saf.org

Index

Page numbers in boldface are illustrations.

About the Author

Ruth Bjorklund has a master's degree in library and information science from the University of Washington in Seattle. She has written numerous books for schools and library collections. In writing about the topic of gun control, she hopes to guide readers into a clearer understanding of the pros and cons of gun-control regulations.

The author lives with her family on Bainbridge Island, near Seattle, Washington.